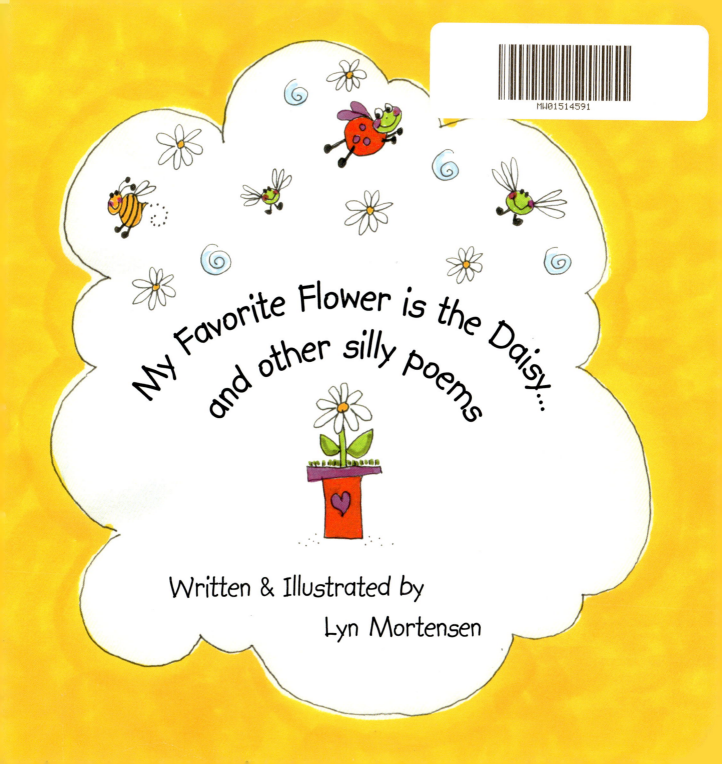

My Favorite Flower is the Daisy... and other silly poems

Written & Illustrated by

Lyn Mortensen

Hello!

Why did I publish this book? I'm following my dream! When I was 9 years old I wrote some silly poems... you'll find them in this book. I remember telling my parents I would be a famous writer some day & publish those poems. Well, I'm not famous, but I have published the poems for you. It only took me a "few" years... you see I'm now 55! I hope you will giggle when you read them, or when they're read to you. I hope the illustrations will bring a smile to your face and a grin to your heart. Remember...

"Follow your dreams,
no matter your age,
when they come true...
see what's on the next page."
Enjoy!

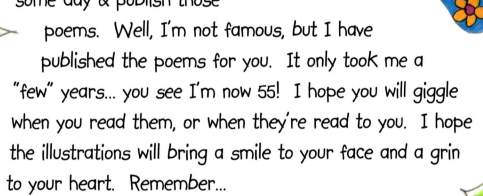

The world is a wonderful place to be!
I'm glad you're you... I'm glad I'm me!

My favorite flower is the daisy
because it looks so lazy.
Everyday in the breeze
it bows it's head... and so do the trees.

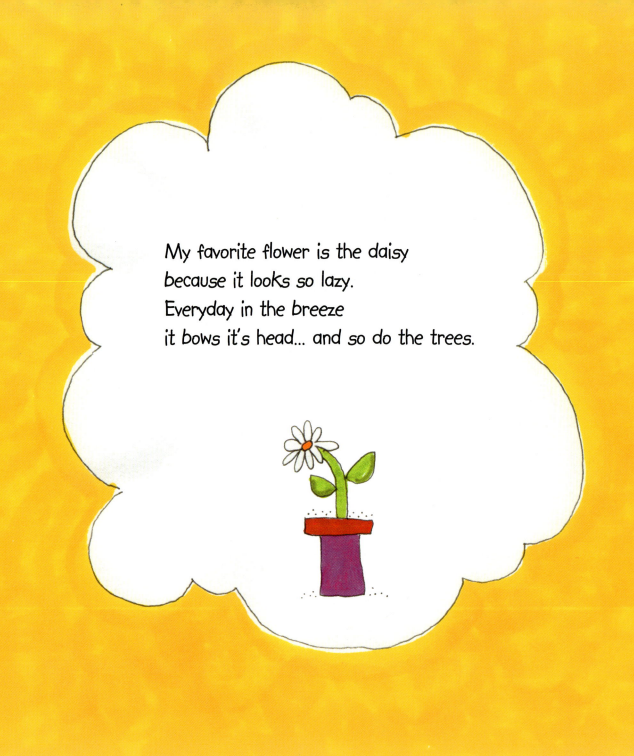

Sometimes when I'm swinging,
in the sky so blue,
I see something yellow...
and you know what it is... too.

Say thank you and say please
for cookies and even cheese.

If you want to come
and have some fun...
let's go run and run.
Don't forget to have some fun!

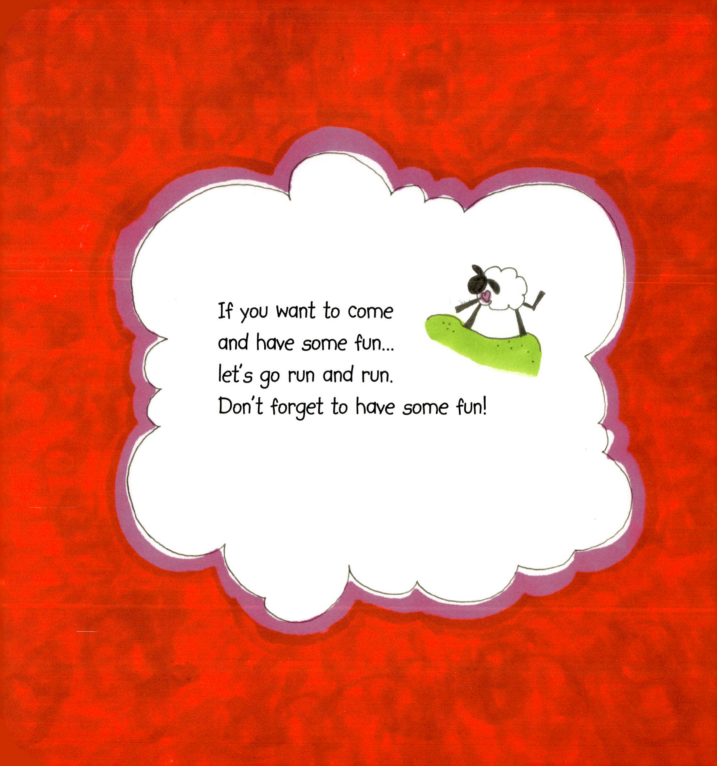

My dog is a friend to me.
I play with him, yes siree.
My cat is very cuddly too.
He plays with my big tennis shoe.
A spider is not a very good pet
because you could get tangled in his net!

I think my boyfriend is real sweet.
Each day at school he looks real neat.
I think he's a very handsome boy
and every day he's full of joy.
He thinks I am a pretty girl.
He says I give his heart a twirl.

I like to dance rock & roll,
but when I do, I do the stroll.
I like to dance, dance the hop,
but when I do I fall down flop!

I like to go shopping, shopping on wings,
I buy trains, dolls & other things.
The stores are very, very nice
but they never sell little mice.
Going shopping is very far...
but we always go in a car.

I love my grandma, she is so sweet,
in fact, I think she's really neat!
I love my grandpa very much,
but he's not close enough to touch.
I wish that they could visit me
so we could live real happily!

It's raining all around the town.
It's raining down, down, down.
It's raining all around the town.
It's raining up, it's raining down.
It's raining up, it's raining down.
It's raining all around.

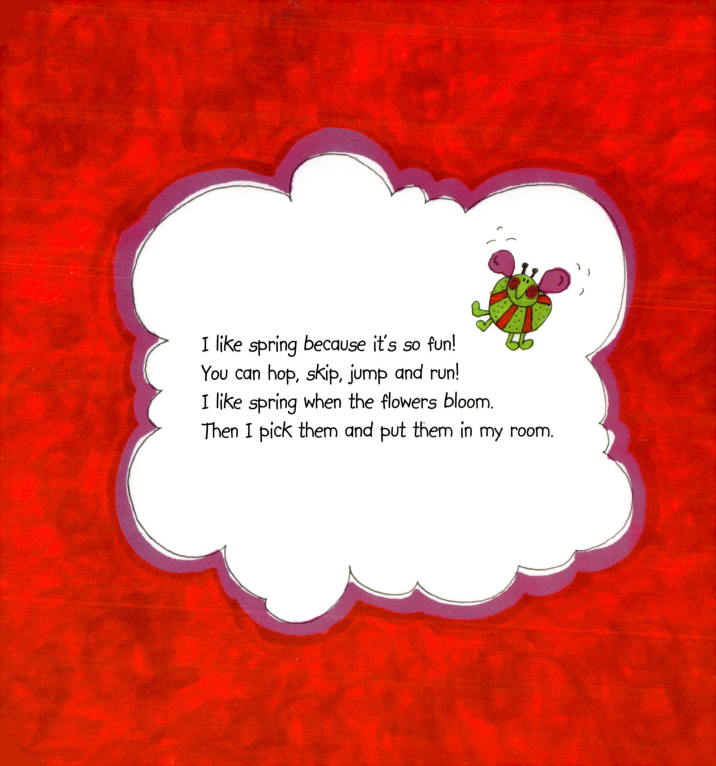

I like spring because it's so fun!
You can hop, skip, jump and run!
I like spring when the flowers bloom.
Then I pick them and put them in my room.

I like gold it makes you rich!
To find it... you have to dig a ditch!

Sing a song every day.
The blues will surely go away!
Sing with your mouth opened wide.
Let the tune come from deep inside!

Up above the sky so blue
I seem to see a picture of you.
That picture seems to be so true
for I love it and so do you.

Under the ocean... down in the deep,
the fish don't ever seem to sleep!

Follow your dreams,
You've got what it takes!
They're waiting for you,
for goodness sake.
Your dreams are worth all the effort you do!
anything is possible... that fact is true!
Follow your dreams, no matter your age...
When they come true, find what's on the next page.
Follow your dreams, reach for a star...
no matter how near, no matter how far!
Follow your dreams, go the extra mile,
and when it's all said and done... you will smile!
Follow your dreams whatever the score...
when one is accomplished...... GO OUT AND FIND MORE!

Write a silly poem of your own!

About the Author; Illustrator

Lyn is an artist whose whimsical work
will bring a smile to your face.
She lives in Colorado with her family,
a crazy cat, "Boots", a big golden retriever,
"Riley" and a few country spiders.

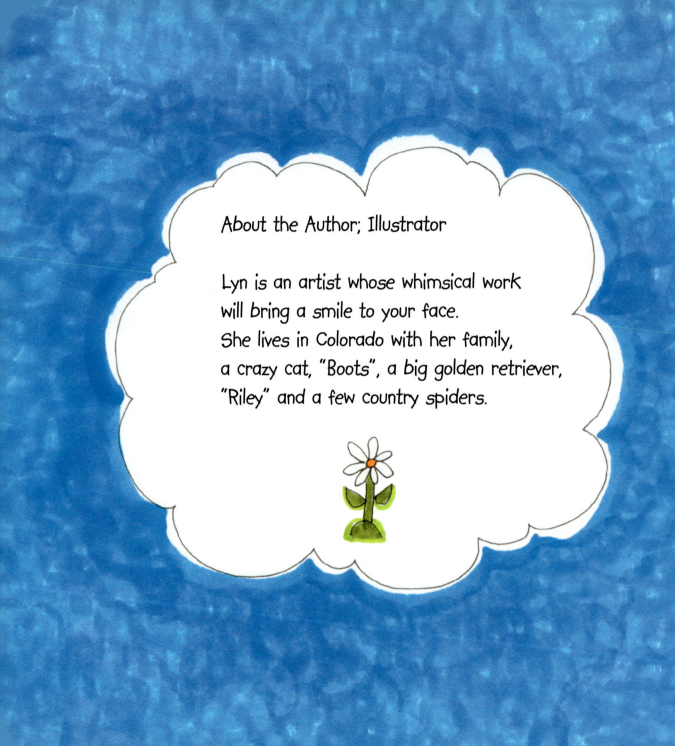

Children... follow YOUR dreams...
Believe in yourselves... and remember...
Anything is possible!

This book is dedicated
to the love of my life,
H.C. Mort..... He gave
me daisies on our
wedding day!

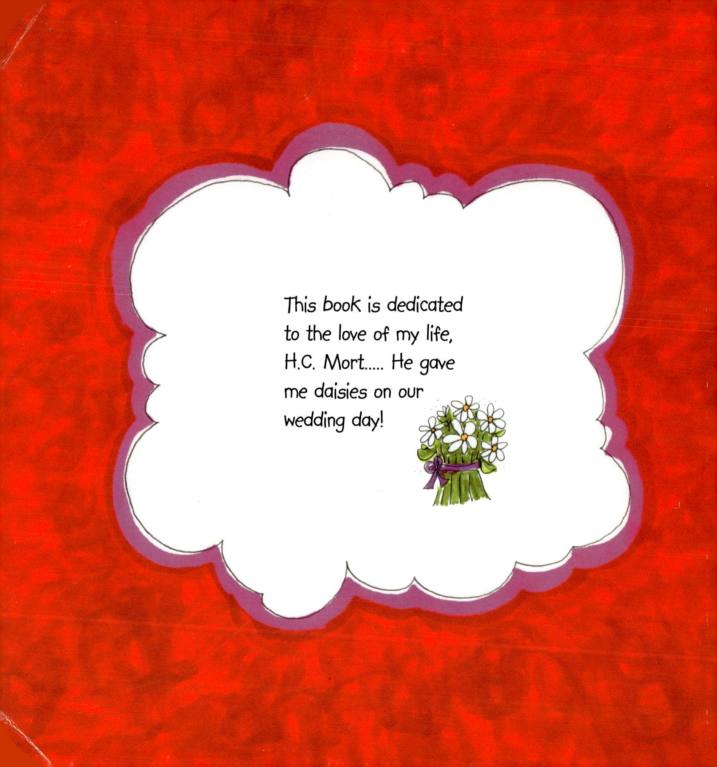